The #1 Rule for Dynamic Leadership

Jason Holiman

ISBN-10: 1720700869
ISBN-13: 978-1720700869

DEDICATION

For the Leaders, from the Led.

CONTENTS

ACKNOWLEDGMENTS

Special thanks to Ryan Johnson. He would like to take credit for this book, but can't.

Chapter One

THIS IS IT

TREAT EVERYONE LIKE AN ADULT.

TREAT EVERYONE LIKE AN ADULT.

The #1 Rule for Dynamic Leadership

TREAT EVERYONE LIKE AN ADULT.

TREAT EVERYONE LIKE AN ADULT.

TREAT EVERYONE LIKE AN ADULT.

TREAT EVERYONE LIKE AN ADULT.

TREAT EVERYONE LIKE AN ADULT.

TREAT EVERYONE LIKE AN ADULT.

TREAT EVERYONE LIKE AN ADULT.

TREAT EVERYONE LIKE AN ADULT.

TREAT EVERYONE LIKE AN ADULT.

TREAT EVERYONE LIKE AN ADULT.

The #1 Rule for Dynamic Leadership

TREAT EVERYONE LIKE AN ADULT.

TREAT EVERYONE LIKE AN ADULT.

ABOUT THE AUTHOR

Jason Holiman is pretty awesome.
Humble as well.

Notes and Personal Reflection

Notes and Personal Reflection

Notes and Personal Reflection

www.ingramcontent.com/pod-product-compliance
Lightning Source LLC
Chambersburg PA
CBHW072034230526
45468CB00021B/1809